PUB WALKS

—— IN ——

The Lake District

Other areas covered in the Pub Walks series include:

Bedfordshire
Berkshire
Bristol & Bath
Buckinghamshire
Cambridgeshire
Cheshire
Chilterns
Cotswolds
County Durham & Teeside
South Cumbria
Dartmoor & South Devon
Derbyshire
Essex
West Essex
Exmoor & North Devon
Gloucestershire
Herefordshire
Hertfordshire
Lancashire
Leicestershire & Rutland
Lincolnshire
Malvern Hills
The Mendips

Middlesex & West London
North London
South London
Norfolk
Northamptonshire
Nottinghamshire
Oxfordshire
Shropshire
South Downs
Staffordshire
Suffolk
Surrey
Surrey Hills
Thames Valley
North Wales
Warwickshire
Wiltshire
Worcestershire
East Yorkshire
North Yorkshire
South Yorkshire
West Yorkshire
Yorkshire Dales

PUB WALKS

— IN —

The Lake District

Ron Freethy

COUNTRYSIDE BOOKS
NEWBURY, BERKSHIRE

COUNTRYSIDE BOOKS
3 Catherine Road
Newbury, Berkshire

To view our complete range of books,
please visit us at
www.countrysidebooks.co.uk

ISBN 1 85306 913 2

Photographs by the author

Designed by Graham Whiteman
Produced through MRM Associates Ltd., Reading
Printed by Woolnough Bookbinding Ltd., Irthlingborough

Contents

AREA MAP SHOWING THE LOCATION OF THE WALKS

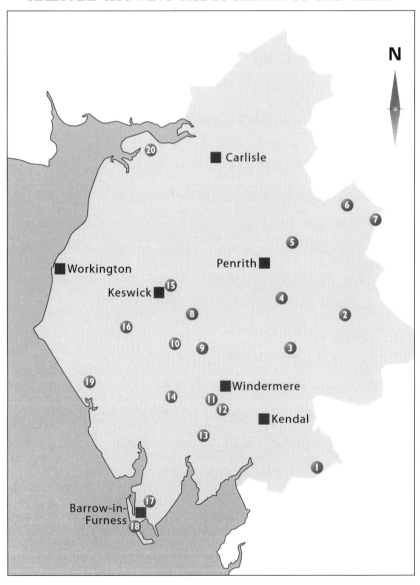

Keswick to the West

To the West and the Coast to Carlisle

PUBLISHER'S NOTE

We hope that you obtain considerable enjoyment from this book; great care has been taken in its preparation. However, changes of landlord and actual closures are sadly not uncommon. Likewise, although at the time of publication all routes followed public rights of way or permitted paths, diversion orders can be made and permissions withdrawn.

We cannot, of course, be held responsible for such diversion orders and any inaccuracies in the text which result from these or any other changes to the routes nor any damage which might result from walkers trespassing on private property. We are anxious though that all details covering the walks are kept up to date and would therefore welcome information from readers which would be relevant to future editions.

The simple sketch maps that accompany the walk in this book are based on notes made by the author whilst checking out the routes on the ground. However, for the benefit of a proper map, we do recommend that you purchase the relevant Ordnance Survey sheet covering your walk. The Ordnance Survey maps are widely available, especially through booksellers and local newsagents.

INTRODUCTION

Born in Barrow but brought up in Askam-in-Furness, my childhood and teenage years were spent enjoying my two favourite Bs – butties and my bike. I still love exploring the Lakes, but now mainly on foot, and I'm constantly surprised by the discovery of new nooks and crannies. During my working life as a journalist I have made television films and radio programmes that look for unusual aspects in the new county of Cumbria. To most of us, however, old Westmorland, Cumberland and the Furness district of Lancashire continue to stir the soul. Wherever the political boundaries are marked following the 1974 changes, the Lake District remains one of the most beautiful and scenically varied regions of the world.

The paths are well trodden, but it is still possible to come across quiet highways and byways and many of these are included in the 20 circular walks described here. The routes vary from 2½ miles to 5½ miles in length and include something for everyone, from family groups to experienced walkers.

I have grouped the routes under six geographical headings, which between them will, I hope, give an idea of the variety of scenery and terrain in the region. I have started with the south-east, around Kirkby Lonsdale and Appleby, an area through which people often speed without appreciating the wonderful walking country on offer. The strolls around Shap and Askham are both beautiful and historic.

Then there is the sweeping and inspiring countryside to the east of Penrith, with a string of either beautiful or atmospheric working villages, all with circular walks around them. Langwathby and Edenhall can be explored from the Settle to Carlisle Railway, the little town of Alston has a historic market centre and a narrow gauge railway, whilst Nenthead was once the largest lead-mining centre in the world.

Quite rightly the Grasmere, Rydal and Ambleside region is regarded as a Mecca for English walkers. Some of the routes can therefore be overcrowded but the three strolls included here are quieter than many. The walk from the Swan at Grasmere up to Alcock Tarn challenging in places but the strolls around Rydal Water and Elterwater are more gentle, with the latter most attractive in winter when bird watchers will be in their element.

Walkers and strollers visiting Windermere and Coniston may well be spoilt for choice, so I have chosen to explore areas on the fringes of the central region. Hawkshead is always busy but the walk towards

Esthwaite displays Wordsworth's country at its best, whilst nearby Sawrey is Beatrix Potter territory. The stroll here leads down to the shores of Windermere and the ferry. Haverthwaite, with its steam railway, is set on the river Leven as it flows swiftly out of Windermere towards its estuary at Greenodd. Coniston can also be busy with tourists but starting from Torver allows the lake to be explored whilst remaining far from the madding crowds.

All walkers know the market town of Keswick because of its easy access to other parts of the Lake District. Set on Derwentwater and Bassenthwaite, it offers a wide choice of gentle strolls and high fell walks. The circuit I have described heads up to the Castlerigg Stone Circle, one of the best preserved and most interesting in England. Signed from the town are a number of lakes including Ennerdale, Haweswater and Crummock Water, which all offer circular walks. The choice was not easy but Buttermere is without doubt beautiful and was a favourite spot of Alfred Wainwright whose ashes were scattered on the bulk of Hay Stacks, which overlooks the lake.

As for the sixth section, the west coast has been the most underrated area in the whole of the Lake District. Dalton-in-Furness was the market town of the monks of Furness Abbey and the brethren also made their mark on Walney Island, which is now an impressive bird reserve. Ravenglass, with its narrow gauge railway is the gateway to the Scafell range of mountains, whilst Burgh-by-Sands has been made famous by Edward I, who died on the marshland nearby. Few realise that this area was also the western base of Hadrian's Wall, which ran from the Solway to the Tyne. The four final routes will give a glimpse of the glories of this region.

What about the pubs? Those who complain that 'things ain't what they used to be' may find these walks something of a surprise. Not so long ago hostelries that were 'nobbut ale houses' have been modernised, many without being spoiled, and you will find plenty of excellent food available. My selection has been made from inns that offer some local produce, because the recovery from the foot and mouth outbreak of 2002 has been slow and the area's farmers need all the help they can get.

Here then are 20 of my favourite routes based close to my preferred hostelries – and I am of the firm opinion that there is nothing like a good stroll combined with a good meal at a friendly pub!

Ron Freethy

① Kirkby Lonsdale
The Sun Hotel

This fascinating route is ideal for lovers of both history and natural history. The circuit starts to the south of the fine market town of Kirkby Lonsdale and follows the banks of the Lune, one of the least polluted of the rivers of northern England. The wildlife is always spectacular as this is otter and kingfisher country and in winter there are regular sightings of wildfowl including goosander and goldeneye. After exploring the town you return to your starting point at Devil's Bridge on a wide track. If you fancy a stroll with sweets for company then a treat awaits you – the Victorian sweetshop in Market Square will provide you with (among many other delights) Uncle Joe's Mint Balls, Everton Mints and Uncle Luke's Sure Fire Cure for a cough, an old remedy which has the added attraction of tasting 'reet.'

Before the new A65 road was built the turnpike road ran straight through the town and in the 18th and 19th centuries, Kirkby Lonsdale was one of the most important coaching stops in the whole of the north of England. The Sun Hotel at 6 Market Street dates from the 16th century and is close to the ancient church. Its porch is supported by pillars and the interior has retained plenty of old charm. The menu is a balance between traditional and exotic, and the choice of beers varied and interesting. Light meals that are ideal for walkers are on offer and tea and coffee are available. Telephone: 01524 271965.

- **HOW TO GET THERE:** Kirkby Lonsdale is situated on the A65 road between Kendal and Settle. It is within 6 miles of the M6 motorway with an exit via junction 36.
- **PARKING:** The town's pay and display parking is usually full on Thursdays, many weekends and during the September Victorian Fair so it is best to use the free parking at Devil's Bridge (GR 614782) located just off the A65 and the walk is described from here.
- **LENGTH OF THE WALK:** 2½ miles. Map: OS Explorer OL2 (inn GR 609788).

THE WALK

1. Start at the car park close by Devil's Bridge. This humpback bridge was not actually built by Old Nick - it probably dates from the 13th century and the Cistercian monks of Furness Abbey were responsible for its construction. Look down from its summit to see the splendid rapids flowing below, the haunt of divers who learn their techniques by exploring the deep pools. On the opposite side of the bridge is a 'bacon butty' caravan used by motorcyclists and this is the place to see vintage machines, some dating from the 1930s. Between the bridge and the well-kept toilet block turn right and follow the riverbank with the Lune on the right. Look out to the left to see the neat little cricket ground, which is often being used on the afternoons of summer weekends. Anglers love this stretch of the river.

2. Continue along the riverbank ignoring the first left turn which ascends into the town passing on old mill.

3. An obvious left turn climbs up a steep set of stone steps and reaches the churchyard. Turn right on a clear path to reach Ruskin's View, passing a castle-like Georgian folly on the left. You could make use of one of the seats and take time to read the plaques on the wall. The meander of the Lune was described by John Ruskin (1819-1900), the art critic, as 'the best view in England and therefore the world'. The landscape painter J.M.W. Turner (1775-1851) captured the scene,

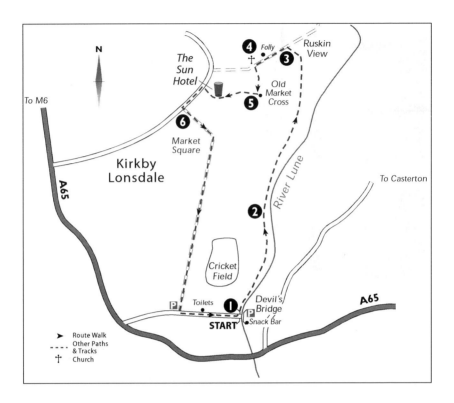

which seems to have changed very little since his paints dried. Return along the obvious path to the wonderful old church of St Mary the Virgin. This was founded in 1093 and some of its Norman masonry remains although there have been several major restorations and additions since.

4. A narrow alley beyond the entrance gate leads to the Sun Hotel in Market Street. In ancient times people travelled for miles to worship and inns were built close by to cater for travellers, their horses and in some cases their dogs, who came with them as protection. From the Sun return to the church and turn right and then left down a narrow flight of stone steps.

5. Descend to the old market square with its cross and interesting set of fish stones. The monks of Furness Abbey owned most of the fishing rights on the Lune and also along the western coast. Their

The Victorian sweetshop in Kirkby Lonsdale

practice was to lay out the fish on the stone steps for the locals to purchase. There was also a swine market here until the 16th century. If people had to travel long distances to worship it made sense to have a market at the same time. Most old markets were situated very close to the church, as was the case in Kirkby Lonsdale. Turn right through a network of narrow old streets full of character, and then turn left onto the main street.

6. Off the main street is today's Market Square with some, but never enough, parking. Here you will find the Victorian sweetshop and splendid little teashops. A wide track leads from the centre of the town back to Devil's Bridge.

2 Appleby-in-Westmorland
The Crown and Cushion

Although since 1974 absorbed into Cumbria, Appleby – famous for its annual horse fair – still feels like a county town and fiercely refers to itself as Appleby-in-Westmorland. Quite right too! This walk, a town and country ramble, starts at the Crown and Cushion pub in Boroughgate and passes wonderful old buildings and close to one of Britain's most historic castles. It crosses the Eden twice and continues on a picturesque meander of this lovely river before returning to the town centre.

In warm weather the outside tables at the Crown and Cushion in Boroughgate are popular as the Market Place, cloisters, church, Moot Hall and the old bull baiting ring set in the cobbled car park can be seen without moving a muscle. Opposite is the Eden Pharmacy dating from the late 16th century and still offering a remedy for those who have 'etten too much'. In 1715 the inn was taken over by the Old Pretender's army and the landlord was not treated well. Treat the present landlord a little better and you will find him to be an expert not only on his own establishment but also on all of the many inns in the town. Locals will not put up with 'nobbut chat' but also demand good beer and substantial locally produced food. The soups on offer are of a particularly high standard and the local lamb and cheese are excellent. I can also recommend the ham and eggs. Telephone: 01768 351595.

- **HOW TO GET THERE:** Appleby is on the Settle to Carlisle Railway and from the station a steep road leads down into the town centre. By road the town is reached along the A66 linking Brough with Penrith. Approaching from Kendal, follow the A685 to Tebay and then take the B6260 through Orton.
- **PARKING:** There is car parking in the town although some areas have disc parking. These can be obtained free of charge from local shops or from the Tourist Information Centre in the Moot Hall. The popular horse fair is held in early June and spaces are difficult to find at that time.
- **LENGTH OF THE WALK:** 3 miles. Map: OS Explorer OL19 (inn GR 685204).

THE WALK

1. From the Crown and Cushion, spare time to stroll through the market cloisters and explore the parish church of St Lawrence. This was important in early Norman times but was badly damaged in 1388 by invading Scots. In the mid 17th century Lady Anne Clifford, who owned the castle, restored the church and both she and her mother are buried there. Look out also for a wonderful organ built for Carlisle Cathedral in the 15th century and brought to Appleby in 1684. Pass through the cloisters onto Boroughgate and walk straight ahead.

2. You come to the Moot Hall, part of which is used as the impressive Tourist Information Centre. The word 'moot' means a meeting place and the present building dates from 1596 but there were probably earlier buildings on the site in Anglo-Saxon times. In 1174 the first market charter was granted. Occasionally the upper storey – the old council chamber – can be visited and the town's regalia can be seen as well as an interesting collection of weights and measures. On display are vessels such as bushels and pecks once used to sell grain whilst liquid containers including gallons, gills and quarts all guaranteed against short measures. From the Moot Hall follow Boroughgate, which slopes steeply towards the castle with old inns to the left and right.

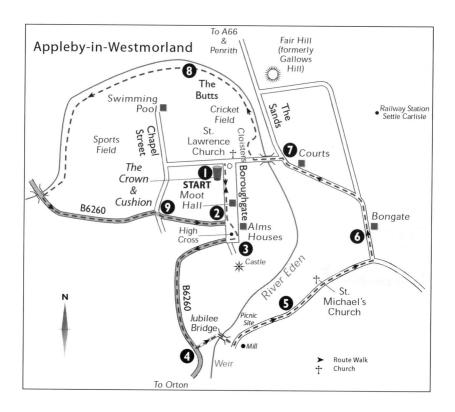

Appleby-in-Westmorland

To A66 & Penrith

Fair Hill (formerly Gallows Hill)

The Butts

Swimming Pool

Cricket Field

The Sands

Railway Station Settle Carlisle

Sports Field

Chapel Street

St. Lawrence Church

Cloisters

⑦ Courts

The Crown & Cushion

⑨

START
Moot Hall

②

Boroughgate

B6260

High Cross

Alms Houses

③

Bongate

⑥

Castle

River Eden

⑤

St. Michael's Church

N

B6260

Jubilee Bridge

Picnic Site

Mill

④

Weir

➤ Route Walk
✝ Church

To Orton

3. Towards the summit look left and enter the tranquil yard, gardens and thirteen dwellings of Lady Anne Clifford's almshouses. These are still occupied by spinsters and widows who live rent free and are looked after by a 'mother', with their spiritual needs provided for by a lovely little chapel. Visitors are made welcome during the day so this gem should not be missed. From the almshouses ascend to the High Cross, which is overlooked by the gates of Appleby Castle. In 2004 the castle changed ownership and unfortunately the former permissive path through the grounds has been closed. This route used to trace the line of the walls of the fortress, which dates back to at least 1092. Instead follow the road round to the right and then sweep left. On the right is the district now known as Scattergate – once Schitergate due to the smell of the long closed tanneries in the area!

4. Follow a steep track descending to the river Eden whose waters eventually pass through Carlisle and then on to the Solway, the

The footbridge over the river Eden

boundary between England and Scotland (see Walk 20). Cross a footbridge that was erected in 1968. This replaced the Jubilee Bridge built in 1887 at the time of Queen Victoria's Golden Jubilee. Look to the right to see the Bongate Mill and its large weir.

Ascend a steep track, passing a row of 17th century cottages on the right.

5. Look left to see St Michael's church dating from the 12th and 13th centuries. It is still a listed building but is now a private residence. Continue the ascent to meet Bongate, which is on the line of the old A66. Turn left.

6. Pass the Royal Oak, a former coaching inn, on the right and then turn left back towards the town. You will walk past old cottages before reaching the police station and the old courts. These and the gaol are occasionally open to the public but there is also plenty to see on the outside. Here are the men's, women's and debtors' prisons plus a mock-up of a treadmill, once human operated, which provided the power to raise water from the river Eden to the roof of the gaol.

7. Turn sharp left over the bridge across the Eden. Look to the right

The annual horse fair at Appleby

to see the river where at the time of the horse fair the animals are washed prior to being offered for sale. The horses are then put through their paces along a stretch of road known as The Sands. At the end of the bridge turn sharp right through a gate to reach an idyllic riverside path. Pass a cricket field on the left and then a swimming pool also on the left, and both on the site of the old gasworks.

8. The meander of the river is a delight and the open space on the left, now used as playing fields, is still known as The Butts. This is where the men of Appleby practised their archery and some did damage to the French when they served in Henry V's army at Agincourt in 1415. Do not cross the next bridge over the Eden but bear left and return to the town centre.

9. Continue over the crossroads and through a narrow alley to the Moot Hall. Turn left to the Crown and Cushion.

3 Shap
The Greyhound Hotel

The ribbon-like village of Shap is situated on the ancient road linking London and Edinburgh. After his defeat at Derby in 1745 Bonnie Prince Charlie spent one night here but was being closely followed by the Duke of Cumberland. Several buildings claim to be his resting place including the Greyhound and The Hermitage on the opposite side of the A6. This walk in limestone and granite country winds its way along narrow lanes through lush green fields and down to a splendid little river. It passes Shap Abbey and the chapel at Keld. The sound of running water and birdsong plus the majestic ruins make the route a joy whatever the time of year.

The Greyhound Hotel was established in 1680 from a farm built in the 15th century. The initials of the original owners, Richard and Ann Whinfel, can be clearly seen high on the wall, and beside the front door is an old milestone. On the opposite side of the road is Green Farm, which once provided the produce cooked at the inn for travellers. Local fare is still on offer today, including the meat which is purchased direct from farmers - the lamb, for example, comes from the farm

19

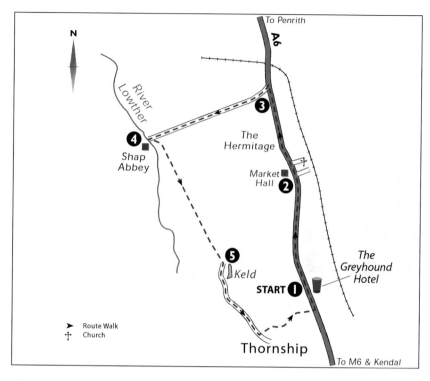

adjacent to Shap Abbey, passed on the walk. There is a children's menu and half-sized meals are also on offer from the main menu. At the rear there is a delightful patio dining area. Overnight accommodation is available in en-suite rooms. Telephone: 01931 716474.

- **HOW TO GET THERE:** From the M6 leave at junction 39 and turn right along the A6 to Shap. If you want to use public transport, the village is on the main West Coast Rail Link. There is also a bus linking Shap with Penrith in one direction and Kendal in the other.
- **PARKING:** The inn has a large car park for patrons. Some street parking may be available and there is also a small car park in the centre of the village on the east side of the main road.
- **LENGTH OF THE WALK:** 4 miles. Map: OS Explorer OL5 (inn GR 565146).

THE WALK

1. Take time to explore the Greyhound with its horse-mounting steps,

20

Shap Abbey, now in the care of English Heritage

old milestone and attractive façade. Carefully cross the busy A6 and explore Green Farm, which was built in 1684 and has kept all of its old world charm. Follow the main road northwards through the village.

2. On the left find the old Market Hall almost opposite the village car park. This looks very monastic, which is hardly surprising because in the 17th century masonry was removed from Shap Abbey and incorporated into the construction. Continue past lots of old cottages kept in excellent repair and a number of hostelries to reach The Hermitage. This black and white structure, which now offers accommodation, dates from the 17th century and is said (who knows?) to have entertained Bonnie Prince Charlie – we should not argue because the building is bonnie enough in its own right.

3. Beyond The Hermitage find a brown sign indicating Shap Abbey to the left. From here onwards there are narrow roads – more like tracks – leading down to Shap Abbey where there is a small car park next to the river Lowther. There are also parallel field paths, which are well marked. From the car park turn right over an old bridge crossing the river. Turn left through a gate and follow a grassy track with a stone wall on the left to the abbey.

Shap Abbey is open free of charge and is in the care of English

21

The chapel at Keld.

Heritage. Shap was founded in the 12th century by the Premonstratensians who were known as the White Canons because of their habits, which were made of undyed sheep's wool. No more than 15 monks were in residence at any one time and Shap was therefore never very wealthy. The buildings were substantial, however, because good quality local limestone and granite were present in abundance. In 1540 Henry VIII dissolved the abbey and sold the stone. Some was used to construct the farm that still stands opposite the ruin. The most impressive remaining feature is the mighty tower, which was built in the 15th century.

4. From the abbey retrace your route over the old bridge. Look for a path to the right climbing up through woodland. The track is easily followed to Keld.

5. Keld is a wonderful little hamlet full of farms, cottages and an architectural gem that is maintained by the National Trust. The 15th century monastic chapel has been re-roofed and is open free of charge. It is on the right of an incline up through the hamlet. Opposite is a cottage and on its door hangs the key to the chapel.

Just beyond the chapel a right turn indicates the cul-de-sac cluster of buildings at Thornship from where a well-marked footpath leads back to Shap.

4 Askham
The Punch Bowl Inn

This walk, which can be enjoyed in all seasons, follows the river Lowther and undulating countryside around the Lowther Estates, owned by the Lonsdale family, passing Askham Hall as you set off, and later the ruin of Lowther Castle as you make your way southwards to Crookwath Bridge. One member of the family - they were known as the 'Yellow Earls' - was the main founder of the Automobile Association and another was responsible for the Lonsdale Belt much coveted by British boxers. The route has stunning views and the variety of trees and flowers is a delight to botanists. There are regular sightings of red squirrels, deer, hares and many species of birds, and otters are occasionally seen along the riverside, especially in winter.

Look at old photographs of a typical Lake District farmhouse and note its sheltered porches and solid stone window ledges. Then place a sign on the wall showing 'The Punch Bowl Inn' and you have the perfect description of this delightful hostelry, which from the 18th century became a popular coaching inn. Here are areas to sit in the sun as well as shady nooks and in the winter a blazing log fire adds to the warm and cosy atmosphere inside.

Don't just read the menu but drool over it and choose slowly. You can, as they say, literally choose 'owt' but local pork and ham is a speciality. At times when the village is a focus for the Lowther Horse Trials the barbecue roasts a whole hog on the spit and then Cumbrians and visitors alike can enjoy a good knees-up. Fishing permits can be obtained by the day on the rivers Eden, Eamont or Lowther, and behind the car park is a neat little caravan site. Telephone: 01931 712443.

- **HOW TO GET THERE:** From the M6 turn off at junction 40, which is almost in the centre of Penrith. Take care turning right and follow the signs for the A6 (NOT the A66). Continue for around 3 miles and look for the signs to Askham.
- **PARKING:** There is no designated parking but there are usually spaces around the large village green. For those enjoying the hospitality of the Punch Bowl there is good parking.
- **LENGTH OF THE WALK:** 4½ miles. Map: OS Explorer OL5 (inn GR 518238).

THE WALK

1. From the Punch Bowl bear slightly left in front of Askham Hall and then turn right. Follow the bridlepath (this is real horse country). Pass between stone walls and look to the right for views of Askham Hall. You may be lucky enough to glimpse the increasingly rare red squirrel among the trees.

Askham Hall is the home of the Lonsdale family. They were resident at Lowther Castle from the 13th century but in 1936 huge death duties forced them to cut their overheads. They abandoned the castle and have lived at Askham Hall ever since. This was built in the 14th century as a pele tower to provide solid protection from raids by the Scots at a time when the two countries were separate and were often fighting each other. In 1574 things were a bit more peaceful and the tower was converted into an Elizabethan mansion. Askham Hall is not open to the public but the views of it from this path are spectacular especially in winter when the leaves are off the trees. One tree found hereabouts is the ash and the word *Askham* is Saxon and literally means 'a settlement by the ash trees'. Continue on the bridleway, negotiating the various stiles, until you reach a minor road.

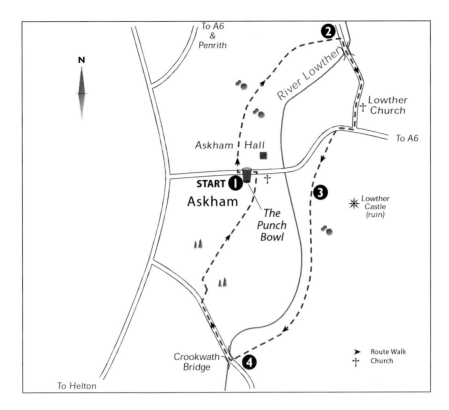

2. Turn right and cross a bridge over the river Lowther. It is thought that the name *Lowther* is Old Norse and means a 'foaming river' - this is a good description especially after rain. Continue down to reach Lowther church on the left. St Michael's is on a 12th century site although today's church is more of a Victorian rebuild. In 1857 the Lonsdales built a mausoleum and former members of the family now lie here in peaceful seclusion. Cross another network of narrow roads, follow an obvious footpath and look left towards Lowther Castle.

3. When is a castle not a castle? The answer is that it depends on what you mean by a castle. The original stronghold was established in the 13th century but by the early 19th century the family wanted a more ambitious home. Between 1806 and 1811 they commissioned Robert Smirke (who later designed the British Museum) to build a 'magnificent edifice'. Now all that remains of the old Lonsdale home is the still impressive exterior.

Follow a track to the right through woodland and across well-kept

Askham's village green

parkland to the riverbank. This leads along a permissive and obvious footpath to the river.

4. Go over Crookwath Bridge and continue along the road. Take a footpath to the right and then right again, signed to Askham. On approaching Askham church, turn left through the churchyard. There may well have been a church here in Saxon times dedicated to St Columba and this was probably rebuilt in the 13th century. The Lonsdales commissioned a new church built by Robert Smirke in 1832 and Charles, the son of the poet Robert Southey, was vicar at St Peter's (the name was changed along with the rebuild) until his death in 1888. From the churchyard follow a footpath back to the Punch Bowl.

⑤ Langwathby
The Shepherds Inn

Langwathby's name translates as 'the village by the long ford' and it retains its original shape with a substantial green surrounded by cottages and farms. This gentle stroll takes us to the estate village of Edenhall with its ancient church and follows a delightful stretch of the majestic river Eden, surely one of the most underrated watercourses in the whole of Britain. Here is excellent fishing, fascinating natural history and spectacularly beautiful countryside. As the terrain is easy and there are no significant inclines this circuit is ideal for families or those 'knocking on a bit'.

There can be few more spectacular settings for a pub than that of the Shepherds Inn, which stands in splendid isolation on the village green. It dates from the early 18th century and was probably a farm before this time. The wooden beams, cosy sitting areas and log fires in winter combine to provide a comfortable feeling of nostalgia. The food menu offers plenty of choice and a special effort is made to ensure that children eat well. The Cumberland sausage is the genuine article and lamb is a speciality. Vegetarians and those who enjoy good coffee are also well catered for. Telephone: 01768 881335.

- **HOW TO GET THERE:** Langwathby is on the Settle to Carlisle Railway. By road from the M6 leave at Junction 40 and then follow the A686.
- **PARKING:** There is parking at the Shepherds Inn for patrons, but there is also a good deal of space around the extensive green.
- **LENGTH OF THE WALK:** 3 miles. Map: OS Explorer OL5 (inn GR 570336).

THE WALK

1. Begin at the village green and the Shepherds Inn. Descend gently along the road marked 'Penrith'. Cross the metal Bailey bridge. In 1968 the sandstone bridge of 1686 was destroyed by flood and the Bailey, which was set up as a temporary structure, is still in use!

2. From the bridge look for an obvious footpath pointing left to Edenhall. Here is an impressive stretch of trout and salmon river. In

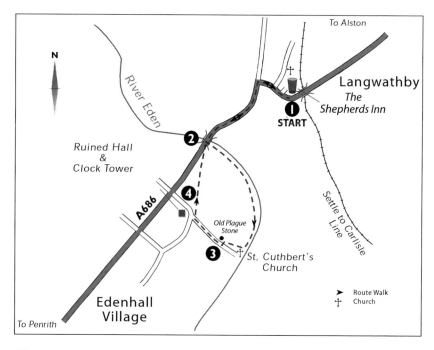

The plague stone at Eden Hall

winter the fields alongside the Eden are often graced by the presence of whooper swans but there are also resident dipper, grey wagtail, heron and kingfisher. Part of this riverside stroll is still called Ladies Walk because it was here that sheltering walls were provided for the visitors to Eden Hall as they enjoyed a gentle meander. Continue alongside the river until a well-marked footpath leads off to the right. Pass through a gate leading to a wide track.

At the junction of the track and the very narrow road stands a large cross known as the 'plague stone'. In the late 16th century more than a quarter of local residents succumbed to disease, thought to have been typhoid rather than the black death. Those suffering from the pestilence left their money soaked in vinegar, and suppliers exchanged this coinage for food.

3. Turn left along a narrow track to the wonderful old church of St Cuthbert, which still looks medieval except for its telephone lines. This was just one of the many places where the saint's bones were rested to protect them from the Vikings. The invaders were not interested in the body but in the treasure with which Christians enveloped the saint's remains. The church was obviously established in pre-Norman times but much of the present building dates from the

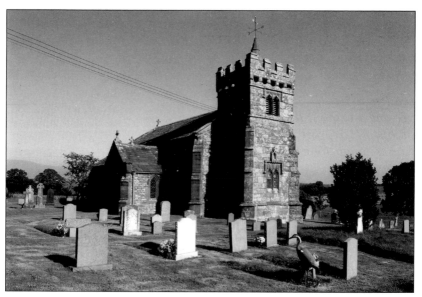

The church of St Cuthbert, Edenhall

12th century and the tower to the 15th. From the church walk back up the track and continue into the estate village of Edenhall, a power base of the Musgrave family, turning right at the road.

The origin of the word 'hall' comes from the Old English *haugh* and Edenhall means 'the flat land by the river'. This description is still accurate today. At one time Edenhall was in the possession of the Bruce family. It was Robert the Bruce who ran riot as the English-Scottish border hereabouts was in flux.

A beaker of 14th century Venetian glass within an ornate leather case, known as the 'Luck of Edenhall', is now kept safe in the Victoria and Albert Museum in London. It was said that as long as the vessel remained unbroken the fortunes of the local Musgrave family would prosper. The glass is intact but a new mansion built in 1821 has been largely demolished. Perhaps the 'luck' should have remained at Edenhall after all. The former stable block, coach house and clock tower is all that remains but the home farm now prospers as the Edenhall Hotel.

4. Continue along an obvious road and then a wide track back to the Bailey bridge. Turn right to cross the bridge and return to Langwathby.

⑥ Alston
The Angel Inn

Lead and water do not usually mix but Alston has managed to become a catalyst that gets the best out of both. The little town with its historic market centre is set in spectacular countryside, which causes tough long-distance walkers to drool about the place. The route followed here, however, is quite gentle and meanders through deciduous woodlands, across surprisingly lush fields and alongside the splendid river Nent with its very much underrated waterfalls. Trout thrive, whilst the birdlife and botanical variation are remarkable. The industrial archaeology encountered as you go is fascinating, and even discriminating experts agree that the vernacular architecture of the area is unique. A trip on the narrow gauge railway along the South Tyne to Kirkhaugh is recommended if you are here in the summer months.

The Angel Inn in Front Street dates from 1614 and is the oldest hostelry in the town. Like many inns of the period it was built to serve the church. The weather can be unpredictable hereabouts and snowed-in

31

worshippers were sure to be catered for. These days both the steak and the mutton are worth travelling many miles to sample. Those who like Continental food will also be satisfied, as will children and vegetarians. The wine list is impressive whilst tea, coffee and sandwiches are pleasantly served in a friendly, cosy atmosphere. Telephone: 01434 381363.

- **HOW TO GET THERE:** From the M6 turn off at junction 40 and follow the A686 signed to Hexham. The road is narrow and twisting so care needs to be taken. It climbs more than 1,500 feet so plan to visit on a clear day. As the A686 passes through Alston look out for the signs to the narrow gauge railway station. Parking is available after the level crossing. All who visit Alston should be aware that the streets are very steep and uneven in places. This, however, is the charm of the place.
- **PARKING:** You can leave your car in the railway car park, which is free. There is limited parking at the Angel but this is for patrons only.
- **LENGTH OF THE WALK:** 3½ miles. Map: OS Explorer OL31 (starting point GR 717467).

THE WALK

1. Start from the railway car park. The line was once a standard gauge route linking Alston to Newcastle. It closed in 1976 but eleven years later volunteers opened a section as a narrow gauge railway and in the summer season (April to October plus Santa Specials in December) visitors should not miss making a trip up and down the line to Kirkhaugh. The return journey takes about an hour and passes through spectacular scenery with the river South Tyne seen at its best (telephone: 01434 382828). The station has been restored to its original splendour. On the site there is a super little café and a shop, and nearby is the Hub Museum (donations welcome), which traces Alston's transport history including railway photographs plus vintage cars, cycles and motorcycles. Opposite the Hub is one of the very best model railway shops; for a small fee the model exhibition is well worth a visit.

Turn left from this site and follow the road up into the town, which is built on a steep slope. Pass the Tourist Information Centre (telephone: 01434 382244) and the church of St Augustine on the right. Opposite the church is the Angel Inn.

2. Continue uphill to the magnificent and canopied market cross, a

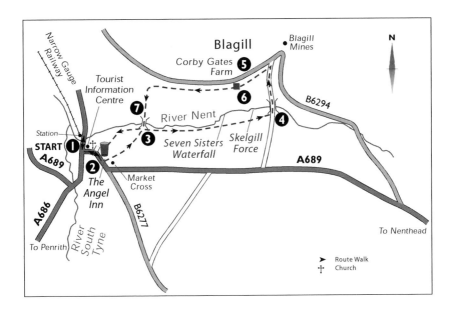

fitting monument to celebrate the fact that Alston, at an altitude of over 1,000 feet, is the highest market town in England. This cross was erected in 1765 with money given by local man William Stephenson who made his fortune and became Lord Mayor of London. There was a substantial rebuild in 1883 and in the late 20th century runaway lorries took their toll. The original memorial stone is now on display in the parish church.

3. From the market square turn left through a network of narrow sloping streets lined with old former shops and cottages, all well maintained. Find a sign to the right indicating Gossipgate. Before the bridge turn right and follow a footpath passing the Seven Sisters waterfall. Alston is so steep that there are several dramatic waterfalls along the river Nent, which is a major tributary of the South Tyne. The whole of this stretch is lined with trees to the right, whilst views up to the left reveal lynchets, which are terraced fields dating from before the Conquest. Birds are abundant here with breeding dipper and grey wagtail, whilst botanists can enjoy flowers such as marsh marigold, grass of Parnassus and an assortment of orchids.

The route is obvious but it passes across a bridge of a tributary stream, through stiles and over fields to one of the best waterfalls in the area. This is High Nent Force but better known to the locals as Skelgill.

4. When you come to the road leading to Blagill, turn left over the bridge and look to the right for the site of the long disused Blagill Lead Mine. The road climbs steeply into Blagill village where the 17th century cottages were used by the families of men who earned their living by mining and farming. It is well worth exploring. Many stone walls were built at this time to enclose stock, with the women and children working as shepherds when the demand for lead was high and the men were busy.

5. From the village turn left and follow field paths. There are field gates here and all the farmers ask is for walkers to close them and keep to the obvious track.

6. Pass Corbriggate Farm to the right. There are deeds for this property dating to 1279 when the settlement was the main 'road' between the Alston lead mines and Newcastle via Corbridge. This was part of the old packhorse route, with the lead horse carrying bells to

The magnificent market cross in Alston

Alston steam railway

warn people that he was passing through. The accompanying men were known as 'jaggers' (but they provided news, not music). Walk through fields alongside wells and approach Gossipgate Bridge, which gets its name from the fact that the water beneath sounds as if it is chattering.

7. Turn right at the bridge and then left towards Alston. The Gossipgate footpath leads into the old stable yard of the Angel. Pass through the entrance, turn right and return along the road to the station.

7 Nenthead
The Miners Arms

The small village of Nenthead, as its name implies, is situated near the source of the river Nent, which is a tributary of the South Tyne. Surrounded by towering hills, it is at a height of 1,460 feet rising to 1,600 feet and the highest house, chapel and Anglican church in England are to be found here. Strangely enough nobody has claimed the Miners Arms to be the highest pub! This walk now leads through green fields, unpolluted streams and neat little woods. It is hard to imagine that not so long ago this was the largest lead mining and smelting area in the world. Lead mining here dates back to Roman times and in the medieval period high quality Nenthead metal was used in the construction of every major cathedral in Europe. This is why the walk should take in a tour of the old workings, as well as celebrating the beauties of a reclaimed environment.

The Miners Arms, which is built of local sandstone, has a fascinating history. It was on the old road used by cattle drovers and later provided rooms for stranded travellers during the bad winter weather. When the Quakers developed lead mining they bought the inn and changed its name to the Miners Arms in 1825. Being Quakers they reduced the rent to almost nothing in the hope that profit would be of less interest to the owner. The teetotal brethren were convinced that their workers preferred books to booze. They therefore set up a purpose-built library, the first of its kind in the country. Previously on the small side, the pub has recently been enlarged with a restaurant extension. This fits so well with the existing building that it does not look new! The menu and choice of beer are as good as ever. Locals love their food, and meat and vegetables produced locally (including leeks from nearby County Durham) are on offer. Dogs are welcome, and just across the road is a children's playground. Overnight accommodation is also available. Telephone: 01434 381427.

- **HOW TO GET THERE:** Nenthead is situated astride the A689 road linking Alston to Stanhope in County Durham. From the M6 turn off at junction 40 and then continue along the A686 to Alston. The road is very steep and there are lots of twists and turns. In Alston turn eastwards onto the A689.
- **PARKING:** There is free parking at the Nenthead Mines Heritage Centre on the opposite side of the road to the Miners Arms.
- **LENGTH OF THE WALK:** 3½ miles. Map: OS Explorer OL31 (inn GR 782436).

THE WALK

NB: In wet weather appropriate footwear is essential for this walk.

1. From the Miners Arms turn left and on the left look for the ornate iron fountain. This was cast in Glasgow in 1877 to mark the work of R.W. Bainbridge, the Superintendent of the lead mines. The local miners subscribed to this project. From the fountain follow an incline passing the lead company's library, now used by the Over 60s club. On the left pass Ivy House, built for the agent of the London Lead Company who supervised the construction of the model village. Each house had, and still has, a substantial garden. On the right there are even older cottages, beyond which a set of the original privies is still standing. Look up to reveal the line of the old road used before the present metalled highway built in the 19th century.

Return to the fountain and cross the road.

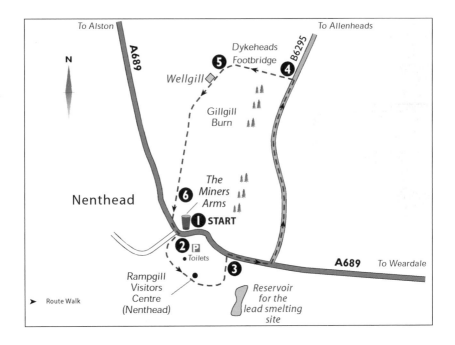

2. At the toilet block turn left into Nenthead Mines Heritage Centre. This has a shop and a very clean and pleasant café. As well as a tour of the site, a visit into the chambers of the old lead mines can be arranged on payment of an additional fee. Children are welcome but there is a height restriction precluding very small visitors. The site gives a clear indication of how huge an enterprise the mining was. A reservoir can be seen and also smaller and now dry dams called hushings – this name derives from the sound made by escaping water as it was deliberately flooded down the hillside to strip the soil away and reveal lead deposits.

To continue the walk, make your way out to the main road (the A689).

3. Turn right towards Weardale and then go left along the B6293 towards Allenheads. Look out for tall posts, which are there to mark a route when snow is standing. The road climbs and to the left are trees marking the line of Gillgill Burn.

4. At the signpost for High House and Allenheads, turn left across a

The entrance to Nenthead Mines Heritage Centre

damp, grassy but obvious path passing through stiles. The view down to the old mine workings is truly spectacular in sunshine.

5. At Dykeheads pass over a small footbridge. Turn left and follow the yellow markers. Move towards Pry House and through Wellgill. In the spring and summer there is a colourful mixture of flowers, some of which, such as spring sandwort, are lead tolerant. The presence of globeflower, marsh marigold and mayflower all indicate that pollution levels are now much reduced.

6. Descend through fields to Nenthead and look out for the substantial houses with gardens and allotments designed by the lead company. On the right of the road is the garage and bus company operated by Wright Brothers. They started up in business in 1914 using pony and traps and are still going strong. Their servicing area is now occupied by remaining buildings initially set up by the London Lead Company.

Continue past the Miners Arms and return to the car park.

⑧ Grasmere
The Swan

This is a Wordsworth walk and the brother and sister were formidable ramblers. I have chosen a testing trek, which involves a strenuous climb to Alcock Tarn followed by a steep descent to Dove Cottage on the outskirts of Grasmere. The effort, however, is worth it because there are panoramic views of Grasmere village and lake and beyond are the breathtaking sights of Rydal and Windermere. All this splendour is against a backdrop of the Langdales.

The Swan, an old coaching house, dates from 1650 and was frequented by Walter Scott (1771-1832) who sneaked off to the inn because his hosts, the Wordsworths, did not approve of strong drink. Poor old Walter was found out when he stopped by whilst walking with the Wordsworths one day. The barman asked Walter if he wanted his 'usual'.

Today the pub is still an unspoilt Lakeland hostelry with log fires in winter, intimate sitting and dining areas and a pleasant garden. The menu is varied but local lamb is usually on offer. Walkers in search of light refreshments are not disappointed. Alternatively one could place an order for a more substantial meal to be enjoyed at the conclusion of the walk. Tea and coffee are also available. Telephone: 0870 400 8132.

- **HOW TO GET THERE:** Follow the A591 between Ambleside and Keswick. Approaching from Ambleside, drive through Rydal and do not turn off left to Grasmere. Continue along the A591 to reach a car park on the right. Beyond this find the Swan on the right.
- **PARKING:** The free car park to the east of the A591. Those who eat at the Swan can ask at reception if they may leave their cars while they are walking. Alternatively, there is also some space by the side of the narrow road leading towards Alcock Tarn.
- **LENGTH OF THE WALK:** 4½ miles. Map: OS Explorer OL7 (inn GR 340084).

THE WALK

NB: Hill walking is involved in the ascent to Alcock Tarn and the descent to Dove Cottage. Walking boots will be necessary for this route.

1. From the Swan turn left along a very minor road. Look out for a footpath sign to the right indicating Alcock Tarn. Follow the course of Greenhead Gill, which is a delightful stream featuring many little waterfalls and is the haunt of dipper and grey wagtail.

2. Approach two private houses. Pass these houses on the right to reach Greenhead Gill. This is a pretty place to stop and rest awhile. Go over a wooden footbridge. Walk to the left and prepare for a long, steep climb.

3. Look out for a bend on the rough track and follow the route of an ancient packhorse trail. Here the winding track gets ever steeper, finally reaching a huge mass of rocks with views along the valley through which runs Greenhead Gill. On the track is a wooden seat bearing an inscription: 'In memory of Tennyson "Tim" Oldfield (1892-1978) who was the author of "*Come for a Walk with me*".' Give thanks for 'Tim' and his seat.

4. The path leads alongside a stone wall and twists onwards and

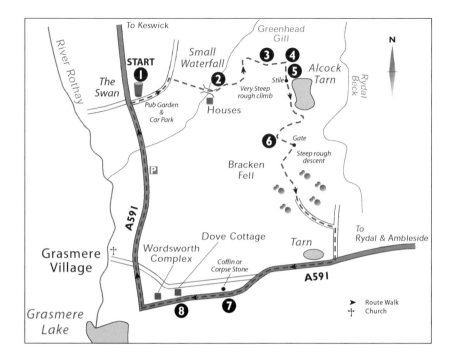

upwards over rocks, grass and a boggy area. Look for a wooden stile over a stone wall.

5. Cross over the stile leading to Alcock Tarn, which is enjoyed in the summer as a swimming area. It is full of reeds and fish and there are many areas that are ideal for picnics. The Wordsworths, William (1770-1850) and Dorothy (1771-1855), loved this isolated tarn. They both lived a long time so their strenuous walking obviously did them no harm.

> *'Here we did stop; and here looked round*
> *Whilst each to himself descends. . .'*

William meant that here was a time to think, but for those enjoying this walk it is certainly time to stop and this marks the highest point of the walk at an altitude of almost 1,500 feet.

From the tarn begin the descent on the obvious route. The way down is very steep and twisting. Care should be taken after rain or frost.

42

Alcock Tarn

6. Approach a metal gate with a National Trust sign on it. Pass through this and continue over Bracken Fell. Here there a number of little streams leading down to Rydal Beck. There are also some well-sited wooden seats. Pass these and descend through a woodland area and close to a little pond to meet a minor road. Turn right and then right again alongside a tarn.

7. Look carefully to the right and find the Coffin Stone. This was on the ancient corpse road, and dates to the time when the folk living on the hills had to make their final journey to be buried in Grasmere or Ambleside churches.

8. Pass Dove Cottage on the right. This was the home of the Wordsworths (brother, sister, wife and children) between 1799 and 1808. The National Trust has done an excellent job in coping with a mass of visitors flowing through the small dwelling. New buildings completed in 2004 and other older structures have been adapted to provide a library, study area, shop and a nearby café which satisfy the every need of Wordsworth's followers.

From Dove Cottage turn right onto the A591 and walk along the wide verge. Continue past the National Trust Regional Office on the right, ignore the two footpaths leading down to Grasmere on the left and return to the Swan.

⑨ Rydal
The Glen Rothay Hotel

This undulating but gentle walk in the heart of Wordsworth country follows the banks of the river Rothay, the shores of Rydal Water and Grasmere and passes a couple of magnificent caves. It can be described as being 'off the beaten track' because tourists flocking to the shrines of Wordsworth and the Lake Poets seldom have enough time to stop and stare at the gloriously rural scene, which has changed little in several centuries. Naturalists love this stroll, as there are resident goosander and kingfisher whilst woodland birds thrive among the gentle slopes clothed in trees.

The Glen Rothay – originally Ivy Cottage and then David's Inn – is a Grade 2 listed building dating back to 1624 and overlooking Rydal Water. Attached is the Badger Bar, which welcomes passing walkers as well as the hotel's guests. Look also for the Oak Lounge, which was built in 1687. There is a non-smoking restaurant, a space for casual dining and a delightfully private beer garden. The hotel takes pride in its chef's specials, which involve the use of Cumbrian produce. Telephone: 01539 434500.

- **HOW TO GET THERE:** Rydal stands astride the A591, which links Ambleside and Grasmere.
- **PARKING:** There is some parking on the narrow road leading up to Rydal Mount where the walk starts. Good parking is available for patrons of the Glen Rothay Hotel and there are also spaces at Pelter Bridge off a minor road as one approaches Rydal from the south. Two good parking areas are located in the White Moss Common area. These are on either side of the A591 and are well signed. There are toilets and usually a caravan serving ice cream and snacks.
- **LENGTH OF THE WALK:** 4½ miles. Map: OS Explorer OL7 (starting point GR 365066).

THE WALK

1. Start at Rydal Mount, one of several homes that William Wordsworth rented during his long life. Many think that Rydal Mount was his favourite and he and his sister found such joy in the garden that he tried to buy the house and grounds. It dates from 1570 and was described as a yeoman's cottage. He did buy an adjacent field for his daughter Dora. It is still known as Dora's Field and is seen at its best

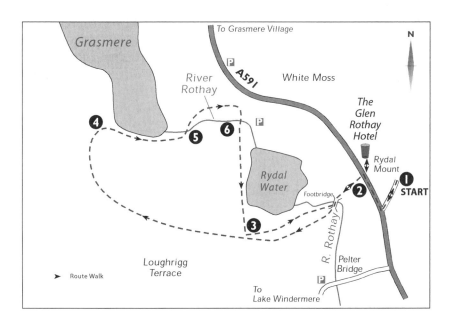

45

Beautiful Rydal Water

when the spring daffodils are in full bloom. The house and gardens are open to the public and there is a small car park on the left of the minor road.

From Rydal Mount descend to the A591 and turn right, taking care as this road is both fast and busy.

2. In a short distance the Glen Rothay Hotel comes into view on the right. Opposite is a gate leading down a set of stone steps to a substantial footbridge. This crosses the river Rothay and is spectacular at all times of the year but especially in the winter when the wildlife is often prolific. At the end of the bridge turn right and follow the obvious winding path. Look down to Rydal Water, once called Rothay Mere, on the right. Here is one of the most tranquil and beautiful of the English Lakes, with the river flowing in, out and through. Rydal is only about ¾ mile long and ¼ mile at its widest point. What it lacks in size it more than makes up for in beauty and there are lots of secluded picnic places along the grassy banks. It is never deeper than 55 feet and is one of the safest of the lakes for swimmers.

3. From Rydal Water the path meanders first left and then right with many gentle undulations. To the left is Loughrigg Terrace. Here are old slate quarries, which have now been reclaimed by nature, and 'Rydal Caves' is an ideal name for them. They now look very natural. From the terrace, spectacular views of Grasmere come into view. Look out for the cone shape of Helm Crag and to the right of this, Dunmail Raise. This is named after a mid 10th century warlord named Dunmail, the last of the kings of Old Cumberland.

Walk through trees and descend gently through a series of gates. You then pass the National Trust Warden's cottage.

4. Turn right, signed 'Lake, White Moss and Rydal' and reach the shores of Grasmere. Larger than Rydal, Grasmere is in complete contrast to the smaller lake but has its own individual charm. This walk only flirts with the village and manages to avoid the tourist crush. The original name was Gris Mere - a place where the Scandinavians kept pigs in the woods that still line the lake. Grasmere's vital statistics are: length 1 mile, width 0.4 mile, depth 75 feet. Follow a path along the shingle shore of the lake and then alongside the river Rothay.

5. Cross a footbridge over the river and turn right along an obvious path. Just before a substantial car park at White Moss Common, turn right over another footbridge.

6. Bear left. Follow the pretty walk lined with trees on the right and Rydal Water on the left. At a junction of two tracks bear left and retrace the route over the footbridge and up to the A591 to return to the start of the walk.

⑩ Elterwater
The Britannia Inn

Elterwater was known to the Scandinavians as Elpt Vatn, which translates as Swan Lake. It is usually the first of the lakes to be visited by whooper swans in winter. The small shallow stretch of water, around ¾ mile in length, is never deeper than 50 feet and its bordering vegetation provides a perfect habitat not only for swans but also for other migratory species of wildfowl. This is an easy walk with wonderful views of the Langdales and only gentle undulations. Those who enjoy waterfalls will find not just one stretch of tumbling cascades but two, adding to the many fascinating features you will encounter on this stroll.

From the 18th to the late 20th century the Britannia Inn was a popular alehouse for quarrymen and workers at the gunpowder works in and around Elterwater village. These days it still one of the busiest hostelries in the area whatever the time of the year. The beer garden is well patronised in warmer weather whilst the interior of the inn is warm and welcoming at times of wind and rain and especially in frost and snow. The main menu, choice of beers and wine list are comprehensive and there is a good choice of bar snacks. Telephone: 01539 437210.

- **HOW TO GET THERE:** From the A593 between Ambleside and Coniston reach Skelwith Bridge. Turn westwards onto the B5343 and follow this to Elterwater.
- **PARKING:** There is a pay and display car park in the village and also on a large open green area close to the Britannia Inn.
- **LENGTH OF THE WALK:** 5 miles. Map: OS Explorer OL7 (car park GR 331048).

THE WALK

NB: At times of melting snow or heavy rain the track beside Great Langdale Beck can become muddy and appropriate footwear needs to be worn.

1. Begin at Elterwater village, which was once the centre of a huge charcoal and gunpowder industry. Any timber can be used to produce charcoal but the highest quality comes from the juniper tree, which

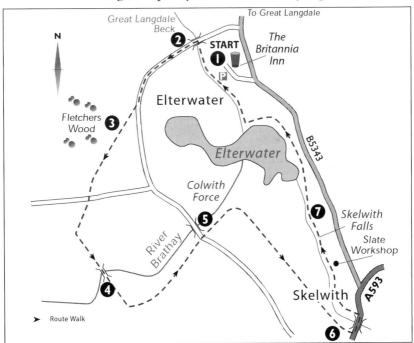

Mute swans on Elterwater

grows well in the area. By the 18th century the industry was in full swing and Elterwater's gunpowder works did not close until the late 1920s. These days local people live happily with a balance between tourism and the slate quarrying that is still carried out here.

Head out of the village towards Great Langdale Beck. Turn left at the bridge and follow the right bank. Above you are the wonderful backdrops of the Langdales. The region was once, and still is to some extent, sheep country and this is reflected in the design of the buildings, many of which date back to the 18th century. Look out for spinning galleries built out on stone steps from cottages to increase height in order to catch the last rays of sunlight.

2. Turn left over a bridge and follow a narrow road for about ½ mile.

3. Look out for a sign opposite Fletcher's Wood and leading off to the right. Who was Fletcher? In medieval times every male needed to use a bow and arrow. We still have surnames of Bowman and Archer whilst a fletcher was a skilled artisan who fixed feathers onto the flight of an arrow. Continue on the obvious undulating path through stiles and gates. Cross a minor road and then the river Brathay.

4. After the Brathay turn left along a footpath signed to Colwith and Skelwith. Cross over a minor road. The route passes through trees to Colwith Force, the latter word simply being Old Norse for a waterfall.

The Skelwith Falls

There are few approaches to beat Colwith. The path descends steeply to a 65 ft cascade set in a rocky ravine and sheltered by trees. It looks and sounds at its best following heavy rain or after a period of snow melt. Colwith until 1974 formed the old county boundary between Lancashire and Westmorland.

5. Follow the obvious track signed 'Elterwater' to Skelwith Bridge.

6. Turn left and then right through a slate workshop and along a narrow track to the second waterfall. What Skelwith lacks in height (only 20 ft) it more than makes up for in volume. Water from the Langdales crashes down towards Windermere. Two small iron footbridges provide excellent places to stand close to the water and enjoy the sounds and sights. You cannot, however, cross these bridges, they are just viewing points.

7. Keep the river on the left along an undulating track whilst straight ahead are spectacular views of the Langdales. This is also the place to see resident mute swans gliding gracefully from Elterwater and along the river. Pass through gates and stiles and amidst woodland to approach Elterwater, which looks at its best when overlooked by a backdrop of the Lake District's most impressive mountains. Follow a solid track. Cross a substantial wooden footbridge and follow an easy stretch of level walking leading back into Elterwater village.

⑪ Hawkshead
The Queen's Head

Whatever the time of the year Hawkshead is busy but this gentle stroll finds undiscovered little paths, extensive woodlands and tiny rippling streams all full of wildlife. Open areas reveal splendid views of Esthwaite, one of the most underrated of the lakes. This is unspoiled Wordsworth country that is literally within a stone's throw of the centre of Hawkshead.

Set in the heart of the village, in Main Street, about 300 yards from the car park, the Queen's Head has been an integral part of Hawkshead since the 16th century. Here are oak beams, stone flags and open fireplaces. The variety of real ales is a wonder to behold but the menu is the real triumph of the Queen's – a meal fit for a king. You will find local pheasant, trout from nearby Esthwaite, locally cured hams, Herdwick lamb and assorted cheeses from Buttermere and the Lythe valley. When you have enjoyed your walk and sampled this menu, which also has vegetarian dishes on offer, you may feel too tired to go home. Why not try a night in one of the en suite rooms? Telephone: 01539 436271.

- **HOW TO GET THERE:** From Coniston the best and most scenic route is along the B5285; from Ambleside via the B5286. From Windermere cross by the ferry and pass through Far and Near Sawrey and along the B5285 to Hawkshead. From the M6 the busiest of the traffic can be avoided by turning off at junction 36 and taking the A590 to Newby Bridge. Turn right and then left over the bridge and follow a minor road past Lakeside and alongside Esthwaite to Hawkshead.
- **PARKING:** Because of Hawkshead's popularity a one-way traffic system operates but there is a well-marked pay and display car park in the centre.
- **LENGTH OF THE WALK:** 4 miles. Map: OS Explorer OL7 (starting point GR 353980).

THE WALK

1. From the car park, toilets and the splendid Tourist Information Centre find a narrow sloping track up to Hawkshead Grammar School. This has a Wordsworth connection but even without this accolade the institution would have merit in its own right. It can be visited at a very modest cost. It was founded in 1588 by Edwin Sandys, the Archbishop of York, who was born at Esthwaite Hall on the banks of that attractive stretch of water. On the outside wall of the school is a sundial dated 1675 and set up in memory of the founder. The school had an excellent academic record and sent many scholars to Cambridge, including William Wordsworth.

2. From the school ascend the gentle slope to the parish church of St Michael and All Angels.

> *I saw the snow-white church upon the hill*
> *Set like a throned lady sending out*
> *A gracious look over her domain . . .*

These lines were written by Wordsworth on his return from Cambridge in 1788 but the white limewash has now gone to reveal the natural colour of the local stone. The church dates from the late 15th century, with the massive tower being the oldest structure. Inside are memorials to the Sandys family and to Sir Thomas Rawlinson who was Lord Mayor of London in 1706. Allow plenty of time to explore St Michael's before proceeding uphill.

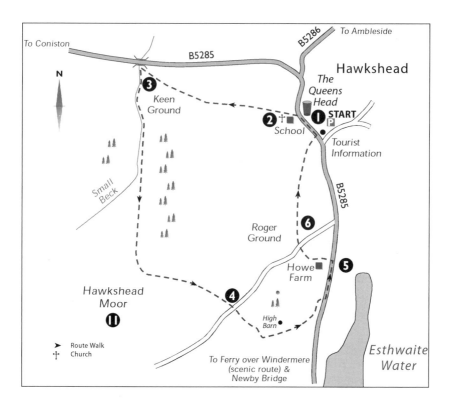

3. Pass through gates until a signpost to the left indicates a footpath to Roger Ground. This passes through Keen Ground. The word Ground has great significance and indicates that there were small settlements there. The area to the left indicates the ownership of the Keens whilst to the right is a very attractive small beck. Walk along a hedged and easy to follow track with mainly conifer woodlands to the right and left. To the right is Hawkshead Moor and you pass a tiny tarn, also on the right.

4. Cross a minor road and continue on to the High Barn area and then turn left for a short distance along the road linking Newby Bridge with Hawkshead.

5. Just beyond Howe Farm a track leads to the left. Soon bear sharp right to reach the hamlet of Roger Ground. Time should be taken here to enjoy the splendid views of Esthwaite Water. This measures 1½ miles by ½ mile and the margin is a tangle of alder and reed, which together

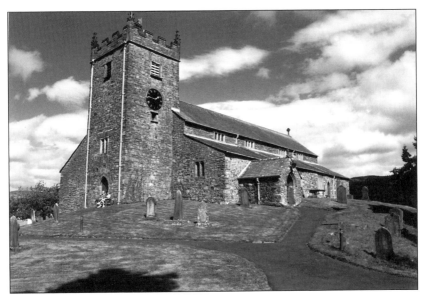

The 15th century church at Hawkshead

offer a wonderful habitat for wintering birds. Until the dissolution of Furness Abbey in 1536 the monks used Esthwaite as a fish farm. There is nothing new under the sun and the water still functions as a fish farm to this day – as the menu from the Queen's Head proves. The monks also had a substantial farm (called a grange) in Hawkshead.

6. Cross a minor road. The final stretch into Hawkshead is a delight for those who love unspoiled English countryside. This is the place to read Wordsworth not as an academic exercise but in a deep appreciation of the joys of nature:

> *Upon a slope above the village school,*
> *And there, along the bank, when I have pass'd*
> *At evening, I believe that often times*
> *A full half-hour together I have stood*
> *Mute . . .*

All should copy Wordsworth. This stroll should be enjoyed in silence except for natural sounds and should never be rushed!

⑫ Far Sawrey
The Sawrey Hotel

This walk, which is ideal for families, leads through Beatrix Potter country and gives an opportunity to visit her home, Hill Top, if you are here in the summer months. It also follows the banks of Lake Windermere and provides idyllic views of wildlife and of boats, both private and commercial, as well as large and small. Part of the circuit passes through quiet mixed woodlands with the distinct chance of spotting the increasingly threatened red squirrel. This is the area that inspired Beatrix Potter to write her stories – and it continues to inspire naturalists today.

The Sawrey Hotel today consists of three sections with the original building, which dates back to at least 1700, in the centre. The old stables were converted into a bar in 1971 and named the Claife Crier. This refers to the ghost of a Furness Abbey monk whose mission in life was to save 'fallen women'. Apparently he saved some women for himself but one girl refused him and he died crying in disappointment. One stormy night the ferryman of Windermere mistook the cry of the monk's ghost for a potential customer. When he returned his hair was white and he never spoke again.

The internal structure of the hotel is of interest and is said to contain timbers from ships that foundered on the old Cumberland coast. It may well be just folklore but some locals believe that wood from wrecked vessels of the Spanish Armada is here too.

The food, which has a local focus, is excellent and the Hikers' Lunch is always popular. There are healthy children's options and the choice of sweets is varied and worth travelling miles to sample. Overnight accommodation is also available. Telephone: 01539 443425.

- **HOW TO GET THERE:** From Windermere and Kendal follow the signs for the car ferry. Cross on this and follow the signs for Hawkshead. From Newby Bridge follow signs for Hawkshead, driving through Lakeside and passing the YMCA complex on the right. Sawrey and the ferry are also signed to the right. The Sawrey Hotel is reached via minor roads.
- **PARKING:** There is roadside parking in the area whilst the hotel has a large car park for its customers.
- **LENGTH OF THE WALK:** 5 miles. Map: OS Explorer OL7 (inn GR 378954).

THE WALK

1. From the Sawrey Hotel descend and turn left at Far Sawrey post office along what is called a minor road. Lake District minor roads are better described as minute. Pass through the village noticing the 19th century parish church, St Peter's, away to the left. Then turn right onto an obvious footpath. This leads through fields and gates. Turn sharp left at a sign indicating Near Sawrey and Hill Top. This is a permissive footpath maintained by the National Trust. The path meets yet another narrow road.

2. Turn left and reach a tiny parking area on the left and Hill Top on the right. This is hidden among trees and becomes quite congested during the season (the property is only open from April to October) but those who love Beatrix Potter cannot afford to miss it (telephone: 01539 436269).

Helen Beatrix Potter (1866-1943) was born in Kensington and soon became recognised as an artist specialising in natural history. She

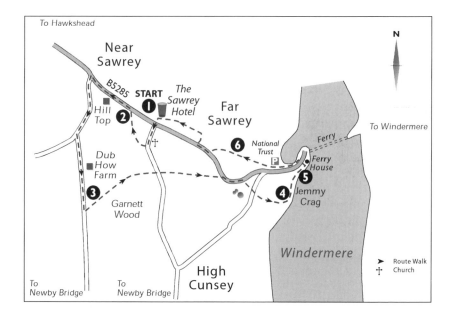

worked for the Natural History Museum and illustrated *Wayside and Woodland Fungi* published by Frederick Warne. When she began to publish children's stories, which she funded herself, Frederick Warne soon realised the sales potential. By 1905 her royalties allowed her to buy Hill Top Farm and for the rest of her life she bred Herdwick sheep. In 1913 she married William Heelis, a Hawkshead solicitor. At her death Beatrix left her house and lots of land to the National Trust.

From Hill Top turn left onto a minor road signed to Lakeside and the YMCA. Bear left at the next junction, continuing along the road and passing Dub How Farm.

3. Look for a footpath leading left into the splendid Garnett Wood, which looks a treat in the autumn. Climb a gentle slope and cross a stile into a field. Follow an obvious terraced track and meet a minor road. Turn left and then immediately right and continue, with the church on the left, to rejoin the B5285 south-east of Far Sawrey.

4. After crossing the road, the footpath turns left alongside the lake at a point close to Jemmy Crag. Here are extensive reed beds, attractive to roosting and nesting birds. Resident kingfishers, reed buntings and

One of the many pleasure boats that operate on Windermere

tufted ducks can also often be spotted. Pass Jemmy Crag and then once more approach the road.

5. Pass Ferry House on the right and then reach the Windermere Car Ferry, which runs a regular service throughout the year. Ferry House was once an inn with a resident boatman who was on hand to row passengers over the lake. In 1929 the inn was bought by the Fresh Water Biological Association, which soon became world famous for its ecological research. This fundamental research is still being conducted and the English Lake District has been a working laboratory for more than 75 years!

Take time to enjoy the comings and goings of the ferry and the pleasure boats that cross its wake. When you are ready to leave, find a path opposite Ferry House. Turn right through a gate. Turn left through another substantial gate and to the right find a National Trust permissive footpath sign indicating Near Sawrey and Hill Top.

6. Pass a ruinous pile known as the station. This dates back to the days of Victorian tourists who liked to be told where to view their beauty spots. From the station descend a paved track. Turn right, passing a car park and continuing through mixed woodlands. Time should be taken at this point because here is one of the few places remaining in England where native red squirrels can be seen. The track reaches a road. Cross this and then in a short distance turn right onto another pleasant footpath. Continue to Far Sawrey and the starting point.

⑬ Haverthwaite
The Angler's Arms

A major part of this varied route is alongside the swift flowing river Leven, here at its halfway point between Windermere and its estuary at Greenodd. It passes through extensive woodlands, which were once at the heart of the charcoal and the associated iron smelting industry. Here too is what was once one of the largest gunpowder works in Britain. The circuit allows visitors to both enjoy fascinating industrial archaeology and to marvel at nature's ability to heal the wounds caused by these early rural-based industries. There is also the added bonus of a steam railway, which runs parallel to the river and accompanies your walk.

Everyone remembers catching their first salmon and sinking their first pint. This happened to me on the same day, with the fish caught in the Leven and the pint drunk at the Angler's Arms! This is still a grand pub and looks quite rural despite the fact that it was built to serve the needs of workers around 1780. At this time there was an iron foundry and a gunpowder works close by. The interior retains its original layout, with

60

plenty of nooks and crannies, and there is a neat little garden area at the front.

The menu offers good plain food including grills, steaks and succulent gammon, with a choice of fish always available. There are also vegetarian options. Telephone: 01539 531216.

- **HOW TO GET THERE:** From Newby Bridge at the bottom of Windermere follow the A590 westwards. After a sign indicating Backbarrow on a very fast stretch of dual carriageway, Haverthwaite is signed to the left. Almost opposite is the Lakeside and Haverthwaite Steam Railway, the starting point for the walk. Those who get their timing right can relax and enjoy a quiet return journey on the train to Windermere, linking with the lake steamboats.
- **PARKING:** There is an extensive car park at the station and at the entrance is an honesty box for those who park. Visible on the opposite side of the A590 is the Angler's Arms, which was on the old main road before the construction of the bypass. This stretch of road is not busy and offers another parking option.
- **LENGTH OF THE WALK:** 3½ miles. Map: OS Explorer OL7 (starting point GR 350843).

THE WALK

1. The Lakeside and Haverthwaite Railway (telephone: 01539 531594) runs a steam and diesel service along a 3½ mile track and links with the steamer terminus on Lake Windermere. There is a restaurant and tearoom on the station and this is open from Easter to October but also at other busy periods. From the station take care crossing the busy A590 and bear right to the Angler's Arms.

2. Descend steps from the pub, turn right and follow a sweeping bend. Turn left along a footpath between buildings and through a field onto the banks of the fast flowing river Leven.

3. At Low Wood Bridge, turn left over the river and then left again along a minor road into the hamlet of Low Wood. Down to the left is a group of very well maintained allotments.

4. Bear left and then right from the allotments. The track leads to the substantial buildings of what was once a huge gunpowder works.

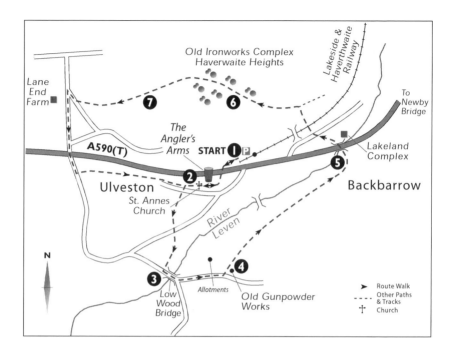

These are now occupied by a variety of craft and industrial units. The gunpowder works were established in 1799 and only finally closed in 1935. Look for the splendid clock tower, which once housed the offices, and still in a good state of repair are the old saltpetre and charcoal refineries. Find a bridlepath alongside the river and through woods, which were once coppiced to produce charcoal.

5. The track leads through a tunnel beneath the A590 and down to the Lakeland Complex – a mixture of time-share, fitness club and a restaurant. These buildings have been wonderfully restored from what was once a complex of mills producing dolly blue, which dyed both the water of the Leven and also those who worked in the mills.

Look to the left and right to see the river swirling beneath the bridge. Here is one of the most popular rapids in Britain for canoeists to practise their skills. Turn left over the bridge and look for a path up to the right. Cross the railway line and ascend into a large area of woodland.

6. Look out for remnants of the historic iron-smelting furnace. The

The Lakeside and Haverthwaite Railway

Backbarrow Ironworks operated from 1698 until 1967 and initially it demanded huge volumes of timber for the charcoal. This stretch passes through these once carefully coppiced woodlands and over Haverthwaite Heights. Keep a close eye open for what remains of some of the charcoal burners' huts and pitsteads. These days the trees have been allowed to mature and there are fine specimens of oak, ash, yew and even a few non-native conifers. There are also a number of alders, which thrive in some of the wetter areas.

7. Descend a winding track and then between walls and trees to Lane End farm which stands astride a minor road linking Haverthwaite with Bouth. Follow this road for about ½ mile.

8. From Lane Ends take care when crossing the A590 and follow a stile through a gate leading to the old road, to the left of which is St Ann's church. Continue on the old road, passing the Angler's Arms on the right, and return to the railway station.

⒕ Torver
The Church House Inn

On days when Coniston is overflowing with visitors the village of Torver to the south provides something of a quiet haven. This gentle stroll leads around two extensive areas of common land and close to granges (or farms) established by the monks of Furness Abbey in the 14th century. The walk also follows the bank of Coniston Water, where the abbey once had fishing rights.

The name of the excellent Church House Inn is something of a misnomer because the church of St Luke's is Victorian. There was formerly a chapel in the area but the building may well date back at least to the 15th century. Many historians look at the inn and point out that the long narrow building has a distinct Viking plan. Once inside, you can marvel at the dark old beams and soak up the ancient atmosphere, especially when an open fire is blazing on cold days.

There is nothing ancient about the extensive menu, and lovers of traditional Cumbrian food will not be disappointed. Coniston-reared steaks are available and these are served with a variety of sauces, as is the locally produced mutton. The gammon is famous for its quality but there are also vegetarian options and children are well catered for in the main rooms and in the beer garden at the rear. There is a wide choice of beers and ciders plus a wine list worth travelling to enjoy. Telephone: 01539 441282.

- **HOW TO GET THERE:** Torver is easy to reach as it is just to the south of Coniston on the A593 Broughton-in-Furness road. Until 1958 a railway ran into Coniston along this route and the new stretch of the A593 now follows the line of the old track.
- **PARKING:** There is some parking on the road close to the Church House Inn, which itself has a very large car park for its patrons.
- **LENGTH OF THE WALK:** 5½ miles. Map: OS Explorer OL6 (inn GR 286942).

THE WALK

1. Start at St Luke's church, which is said to be the successor of a little chapel set up by monks, although not those of Furness. The priors of Conishead near Ulverston administered the chapel and following its dissolution in 1538 the building was consecrated in its own right.

Coniston Water

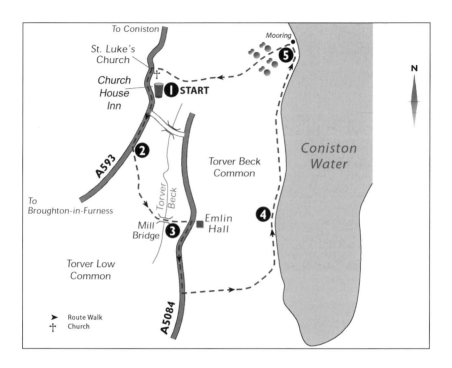

Follow the line of the old railway along the present A593 – don't miss the old stationmaster's building. Continue beyond the A5084 turning and look out for a narrow lane to the left.

2. Follow an obvious bridleway, continuing beside a wooded area to the right, part of the extensive Torver Low Common. These were important free grazing areas for the local people and survived the Enclosure Acts of the 18th century. Approach Mill Bridge and cross Torver Beck. You will see the remnants of an old water wheel.

3. After the beck, follow the hedged footpath to the A5084 and Emlin Hall. This is one of the old granges established by the monks of Furness Abbey and the area still remains pastoral in nature. Follow the road south until a sign is reached which indicates 'Coniston via the Lake Shore'. The path turns right and then sweeps left and hugs the shore of Coniston. This was once called Thorsteins Water, which indicates a Norse settlement and may well account for the design of the Church House Inn. The lake is 5 miles long and at its deepest point is 175 feet.

66

The mooring point at Coniston

4. The path here undulates and passes through kissing gates before descending to the waterside. Look out over the lake to see Water Park beyond you, and Brantwood across on the far shore. Water Park is another of the monastic granges whilst Brantwood was once the home of John Ruskin (1819-1900). Ruskin strode like a colossus over the Victorian artistic establishment and lived at Brantwood in his own brand of splendid isolation. He even refused a grave in Westminster Abbey and preferred to lie at rest in Coniston church.

Continue alongside the lake as far as a mooring used by the National Trust owned boats, surely one of the most historic of its type in the world. The steam launch *Gondola*, now splendidly restored, was built in 1860 as a passenger launch for the Furness Railway Company.

5. Look for a footpath to the left signed to Torver. This leads through extensive woodlands, with Torver Beck Common seen away to the left. On both the Torver commons look out for prehistoric remains including what may be the remnants of stone circles. Pass through gates and dog stiles, across fields, keeping a little beck to the left, and then along a stretch of old railway to the A593. Turn left to return to the starting point.

ⓖ Keswick
The Twa Dogs Inn

This walk is ideal for those with the energy to get away from the crowds that flock to the shores of Derwentwater. In a series of fairly gentle undulations the route leads to the Castlerigg Stone Circle and then over fields and becks to St John's in the Vale church. There are majestic views of two of the Lake District's most atmospheric mountains. Skiddaw rises to a height of 3,053 feet and Blencathra, known also as Saddleback because of its shape, soars to 2,847 feet. The views from the stone circle never seem to be the same, whatever the time or the season, but there is no doubting the haunting atmosphere, which is so typical of this wonderful ramble.

Do not be fooled into thinking that the delightful Twa Dogs Inn is just an alehouse – it is so much more than this. Inside the 18th century hostelry are beamed ceilings and a series of small cosy rooms ideal for eating in when the weather is cool or wet. Outside there is an elevated beer garden to the side and picnic tables at the front. The choice of beers is wide and you will find a well chosen wine list. The menu is both varied and substantial and includes a choice of sandwiches for walkers. Children are made welcome. Telephone: 01768 772599.

- **HOW TO GET THERE:** As a major tourist centre Keswick is signed along the A66 linking Penrith with Cockermouth. From Windermere it is reached along the A591 via Grasmere and Thirlmere. The pub will be found at the junction of the A591 and the A66.
- **PARKING:** Although always busy, Keswick has plenty of parking, some of which is pay and display. Outside town, things are much quieter and there is street parking around the Twa Dogs in Penrith Road close to the junction of the A591 and the A66.
- **LENGTH OF THE WALK:** 5½ miles. Map: OS Explorer OL4 (inn GR 285235).

THE WALK

1. From the Twa Dogs ascend the busy road for a short distance as it sweeps left and right. Follow a very narrow minor road signed to the right and climb steeply to a small parking area at Castlerigg Stone Circle.

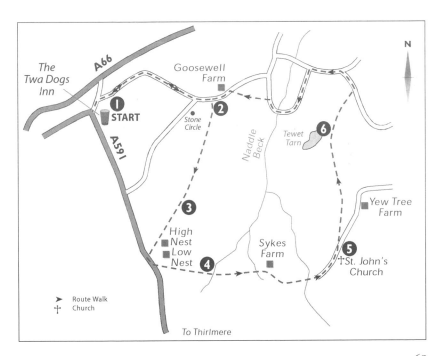

The Castlerigg Stone Circle

2. Pass through a metal gate leading directly to the National Trust's stone circle, which is maintained in excellent order. The circle is some 4,000 years old and inspired John Keats (1795–1821) to write his epic poem *Hyperion*. The 38 stones make up a 100 foot ring with a further 10 smaller stones inside constituting a second ring. Overlooked by the looming bulk of Saddleback the circle is inspirational to all, not just Keats!

From the circle return to the minor road and turn right to Goosewell Farm. A footpath signed right indicates 'The Nest'.

3. Follow the obvious footpath through four fields and pass through a gate at High Nest. The public footpath follows the drive, with the house on the left. Cross a cattle grid and turn left into a field, passing Low Nest.

4. The path widens and then crosses two footbridges over tributaries of the Naddle Beck following well-marked signs for St John's in the Vale church. The route becomes quite steep and rocky, with Sykes Farm to the left of the track. Pass through a gate leading into a

The view from the church of St John over the Naddle Valley

very narrow motor road. Turn left to the Youth Centre and the church.

5. St John's church dates only from 1845 but this remote site had its place of worship from at least 1554. It always looks pretty but especially in spring when it is surrounded by daffodils. In the churchyard is a holy spring, which was probably a focus for pilgrims as early as pagan times. The church is usually open and provides an oasis for quiet contemplation.

Return to the church gate and look for a slit stile almost immediately opposite. Follow the obvious footpath signed to Tewet (Tewit) Tarn. This is the old word for the lapwing, which still breeds around the small stretch of water.

6. At the tarn, Skiddaw can be seen to the left and Saddleback to the right. Prior to the tarn cross a stile and keep the water on the left. Turn right at a fingerpost and descend a grassy track leading to a narrow lane. Turn left, then left and then left again and cross a footbridge over the Naddle Beck. Find a marked permissive footpath owned by the National Trust, signed 'Castlerigg'. At Goosewell Farm turn left, and pass the stone circle on the left. The sun will have moved during the course of the walk so the stone circle will reveal a different light pattern. Enjoy this before descending the narrow road into Keswick to return to the starting point.

16 Buttermere
The Fish Hotel

This stroll is through a tranquil valley fringed by trees, with lush green fields whilst high above are splendid waterfalls. Along the valley are the lakes of Crummock Water and Buttermere, which were obviously joined together in the not too distant past. Buttermere is thus set among some of the best walking country in the Lake District and this walk, which circles the lake, is sure to entrance the naturalist whatever the time of year. In winter sunshine after rain this lovely place is particularly inspiring.

There may be more attractive buildings than the Fish Hotel but not many have a more fascinating literary history – and in addition the fish celebrated is not a common species but one of the rarest in the world. Buttermere became famous as a result of a Victorian melodrama for it was here at the Fish, run by her parents, that in 1802 Mary Robinson, known as the beauty of Buttermere, was seduced and bigamously married by John Hatfield posing as the Honourable Colonel Hope. He was eventually hanged at Carlisle for forgery. Mary's second marriage was happier and she lived to a ripe old age almost unaware of her fame, which was perpetuated by Coleridge, Southey and Wordsworth and acted out on the London stage.

The fish referred to is the char, an arctic species related to the salmon, which became land-locked during the Ice Ages. Potted char still features occasionally on the menu as well as other fish whilst the local beef and lamb, alongside an assortment of succulent sweets, ensure that eating in this historic spot, inside and out, is memorable. Telephone: 01768 770253.

- **HOW TO GET THERE:** Despite the fact that Buttermere is on the tourist trail it is still little more than a hamlet. There are several approach routes but the final entry is along narrow roads so care needs to be taken. From the A66 Buttermere is reached from Newlands, or from the Whinlatter Pass and Lorton via the B5292 and the B5289. Another scenic route is via the Honister Pass from Keswick and through Borrowdale. From Cockermouth follow the B5292 and then the B5289; alternatively there is an A road (the A5086) and a turn off to Loweswater and on to Buttermere.
- **PARKING:** There is a National Trust car park (fee payable) in Buttermere. Because parking is at a premium the large car park at the Fish Hotel is only for patrons and it is easy to see why. Walkers, however, are welcome providing they use the facilities on offer.
- **LENGTH OF THE WALK:** 4½ miles. Map: OS Explorer OL4 (car park GR 174169).

THE WALK

1. Start at the tiny parish church of St James, which is reached by a short but steep climb and entered via a stone porch with views of cottages, farm buildings and Buttermere Lake. When the famous Lakeland writer Alfred Wainwright died in 1991 his ashes were scattered on the mountains overlooking Buttermere and there is a memorial to him in the Victorian church.

2. From the church descend to the Fish Hotel, which has spectacular views on all sides. To the right can be seen Crummock Water. Turn left and follow the shoreline of Buttermere, which is less than 1¼ miles long and never deeper than 95 feet. The whole area is

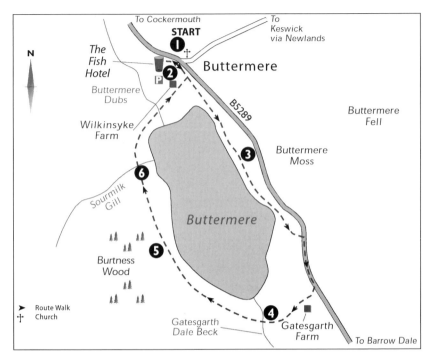

owned by the National Trust and most of this walk is along their permissive footpaths.

3. The path is easy to follow and passes through a number of kissing gates. You walk through areas of woodland whilst to the right there are occasional views of Buttermere Fell including Hay Stacks, which Wainwright listed as his favourite mountain. Where there is one of the best views you will find a picnic area with a seat. Keep to the right where there are other strategically placed benches. Sweep left to reach the B5289 and at Gatesgarth Farm turn right and cross Gatesgarth Dale Beck via a wooden footbridge.

4. At this footbridge bear round to the right and follow the path on the opposite side of Buttermere. Look out for anglers fishing on the lake. Permits to fish are available, and boats can be hired from the village.

5. The route leads into Burtness Wood, which is a mix of mainly native trees but several exotic species are present including some

74

The Fish Hotel seen at its best across fertile fields

splendid specimens of larch. On the ground is a carpet of mosses, some species rare enough to attract botanists both professional and amateur.

6. Cross a footbridge over Sourmilk Gill, which takes its name from the frothing torrent of a waterfall that crashes down the hillside away to the left.

Continue onwards along an obvious track and cross a footbridge over the substantial Buttermere Dubs, which flows out of Crummock Water. Approach Wilkinsyke Farm and then return via an obvious track to Buttermere. On the right are idyllic fields full of grazing sheep and cattle. Away in the distance is a dramatic view of the white painted Fish Hotel.

⑰ Dalton-in-Furness
The Abbey Tavern

Here at Furness, the Cistercians built their abbey, as they always did, amidst unspoiled countryside with little streams used to serve their need for pure water. This interesting walk follows the valley - known as the Vale of Deadly Nightshade because the plant grows in the area - and then ascends onto the limestone plateau of Low Furness and its capital at Dalton. The circuit concludes by passing through woodlands and fields, all once valuable resources for the monks. English Heritage is developing the obvious tourist attractions of the abbey. This will add even more to the popularity of the Abbey Tavern and also enhance the attractions of this stroll through history and natural history.

Although substantially rebuilt following bomb damage in the Second World War, the Abbey Tavern, alongside the ruins of Furness Abbey, retains the atmosphere generated over a period of more than 500 years. The inn, which is on the site of a 17th century manor house built after the dissolution of the abbey, was extensively developed by the Furness

Railway Company in 1847. This is a magnificent setting in which to enjoy a traditional English dinner, and succulent roasts are a speciality. There are also plenty of hot snacks and sandwiches to tempt walkers. An extensive choice of beers and lagers is offered and there is an imaginative wine list. The attractive beer garden is popular in summer, and at all times children are welcome. Telephone: 01229 825359.

- **HOW TO GET THERE:** Once sited directly on the A590 between ancient Dalton and modern Barrow-in-Furness, the abbey is quieter since the construction of a bypass. If you are approaching from Ulverston, Dalton is signed to the left off the new road. Pass through this ancient settlement and follow the signs to Barrow. After a steep descent and a series of sweeping turns find a sign to the left. Go down a steep, narrow road to the abbey ruins and the tavern.
- **PARKING:** There is a substantial car park shared by the abbey and the inn. Beyond the ruins is another large free car park and with public toilets to the right.
- **LENGTH OF THE WALK:** 5 miles. Map: OS Explorer OL6 (inn GR 217718).

THE WALK

1. The Cistercians moved to this site from Tulketh near Preston in 1127. They built well and managed their lands to such perfection that Furness became one of the richest abbeys in the whole of England. It was dissolved in 1537 but the ruins are still extensive and haunting. From the Abbey Tavern a footpath skirts the ruins to the left but it is well worth paying the entry fee to explore the red sandstone edifice at leisure.

2. At the rear of the toilet block of the car park look for a footpath close to the railway line. Pass through a stile and descend to Park House Farm once part of the abbey's estate. Turn left at the yard and pass under the railway line and look for a sign indicating Newton, to continue left along the road.

3. In about ¼ mile you will see a path leading to Bow Bridge. This packhorse span dates at least from the 15th century and was built at a time when the monks kept the highways in good repair to ensure that their trade flowed freely. Ascend an obvious curving track through

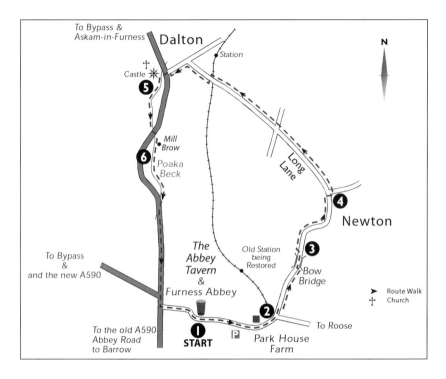

stiles and gates to Newton, which has its own popular inn, the Farmers Arms.

4. Cross the road opposite the pub and follow Long Lane with hedges prominent on either side. There are ponds in the area but these are not natural having been formed by subsidence as a result of iron ore mining. This was begun by the monks but reached a peak in the 19th century. The obvious and very pleasant track with left turns leads to Dalton Primary School. Descend down Cemetery Hill and at the centre of the settlement turn left. Pass the Wellington Hotel on the right.

5. Ascend the road to an escarpment on which stand Dalton Castle and the parish church of St Mary. Both these buildings cast a mellowing shadow on the car park that now occupies the ancient town square. The church was established in Norman times but the present structure is mainly Victorian. Its claim to fame lies in the churchyard, where the famous portrait painter George Romney (1734–1802), who was born in Dalton, is buried. The so-called castle dates from the 14th century and was

The Cistercian ruins of Furness Abbey

built by the monks as a defence against the invading Scots. They needed to ensure that some of their more valuable treasures were kept safe.

On Church Street turn left through some Georgian buildings. Descend to the Brown Cow and an old school, now a restaurant. Follow a sign indicating Millwood, which also dates to monastic times. The mill was powered by Poaka Beck. Keep the beck to the left and then ascend the path parallel to the old A590, now a minor road linking Dalton to Barrow via Furness Abbey.

6. Cross under the road and follow the Mill Brow road back to the abbey.

⑱ Biggar, Walney Island
The Queen's Arms

There can be few, if any, walks that offer such a contrast as this wonderfully remote route. It must rank as one of the most spectacular in the whole of Britain. There are monastic connections, a castle on an island with possible Thomas the Tank Engine connections, a wide assortment of birdlife and botany plus sea views with a backdrop of Lake District mountains. Here also are some of the most magnificent sunsets to be found anywhere in the North of England. The 5 mile circular walk actually begins at the South Walney Nature Reserve, and the drive south from the Queen's Arms to reach it passes a unique series of historical locations.

A close look at the Queen's Arms reveals just what it once was – a typical farm, built on the site of an old monastic grange. From the car park there is the chance to enjoy the architecture associated with farming in an age when there was no specialisation. Each farm was self-sufficient and the skill was in providing a little extra to sell in local markets or to cater for the occasional visitor. The Queen's Arms is a real reminder of this bygone age and a quiet meal here allows the atmosphere of a medieval farmhouse to be enjoyed. The fact that it is so isolated and yet remains a popular place to eat is not only a testimony to its varied menu but also to the quality of the food and drink – non-drivers will enjoy the balance between cask beers and real ales. Telephone: 01229 471113.

- **HOW TO GET THERE:** Walney Island is reached by following the A590 through Barrow-in-Furness. Cross over Jubilee Bridge onto the island. Turn left at traffic lights and keep to main road. Descend and turn left onto Carr Lane. This leads directly to the little hamlet of Biggar.
- **PARKING:** This is not a busy place and there is roadside parking. The Queen's Arms has a large car park for its patrons. Park for the walk at the South Walney Nature Reserve.
- **LENGTH OF THE WALK:** 5 miles. Map: OS Explorer OL6 (inn GR 194663; South Walney Nature Reserve GR 215621).

THE WALK

NB: There are parking points along the narrow road leading south from Biggar to the nature reserve where the walk starts.

Biggar village was originally a farm settlement set up by the monks of Furness Abbey in the 13th century. The brethren fed and drank well and here pigs, sheep and cattle grazed whilst grain was grown and poultry provided meat and eggs. Biggar has not altered much since, although the original strips of land became enclosed by walls and dykes in the 18th century. Follow the narrow road, keeping the sea to the left.

Look out to the left to see the remains of a series of brine wells dating from the late 1890s. A pipe pumped brine to saltpans near the pier at South Walney. Look out to the left to see Piel Island surmounted by what is described as a castle. This was built by the monks to protect their goods brought in by sea. In 1487 an army from Ireland landed on the island but the attempt by Lambert Simnel to replace Henry VII failed. Some think that the Rev Aubrey used Piel and nearby Rampside as the inspiration for the Island of Sodor in his *Thomas the Tank Engine* stories. Continue to follow the narrow winding road, which soon develops into a rough track.

Pass between a pleasant caravan park and a farm known as South End. This was also run by the monks at one time but for some reason it did not develop in the same way as Biggar and is still only an isolated farm. From South End follow the rough track to South Walney Nature

81

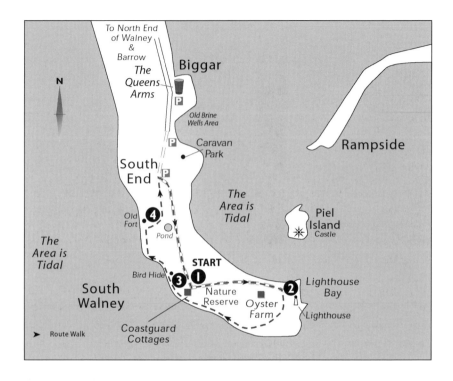

Reserve, which is run by the Cumbria Naturalists' Trust. This is open daily except Mondays throughout the year; a small charge is made and there is a neat little car park and toilets. The warden's accommodation is in the Old Coastguard Cottages and other cottages on the site are available for hire (telephone: 01539 816300). Visitors should be aware that this is a bird sensitive site and dogs are not allowed.

1. Set out on foot from the car park, keeping Piel Island away to the left. Follow the track to the old saltworks and pier and, away in a dip to the right, is an oyster farm. If you expect to buy fresh oysters you will be disappointed – in these algae-rich waters young oysters are reared until they are about the size of a 50 pence coin and they are then sent to other nurseries where they grow to full size before being harvested. The saltworks were developed in the late 19th century but were never successful and closed down in 1909 although there is still plenty of evidence to be seen. Sand and gravel works are still being worked spasmodically and the scrapes produced provide excellent habitat for breeding eider ducks.

Piel Island is dominated by the ruins of a 14th century castle

2. The track sweeps right along Lighthouse Bay to the lighthouse itself, which no longer functions having been replaced by more sophisticated equipment. It was built in 1790 to guide ships importing sugar into Lancaster docks from Jamaica long before Barrow-in-Furness became a port. The lighthouse is still lived in and is in an excellent state of repair.

From the lighthouse look to the right to find a marked path leading through the sand dunes to the sea on the opposite side of the island. In the breeding season there is a mixed colony of some 25,000 pairs of herring gulls and lesser black backed gulls. These take exception to visitors and most people do get 'whitewashed' – so you need to hold a stick above your head and wear a hat and an old coat. If this walk is done in winter it is a much gentler experience, but for the bird watcher it can be spectacular with wonderful sea views over to the Lake District mountains and often beautiful sunsets.

3. Close to the path are views to the right of the coastguard cottages and then a well-appointed sea hide. Here is the place to watch wintering skuas, auks and shearwaters. All is peaceful now but look for the remains of a Second World War defensive fort, which is slowly but surely being washed away by the sea.

4. Swing right at the fort and follow an obvious track to South End. Turn right to walk back to the car park at the nature reserve. Return to Biggar village and the Queen's Arms by car.

⑲ Ravenglass
The Ratty Arms

A circular walk with a difference! Ravenglass with its three rivers of Irk, Mite and Esk, which share an estuary here, has been busy since Roman times. The best and easiest way to explore this trio of little rivers is to ascend to Dalegarth aboard La'al Ratty, as the narrow gauge Ravenglass and Eskdale Railway is affectionately called. The railway, which is mainly steam operated, runs throughout the year with the exception of January and allows panoramic views to be enjoyed over the estuary whilst beyond is the mountain panorama dominated by Scafell and the even higher Scafell Pike – England's highest peak. Allow time to work out the train timetable and then, having arrived in Dalegarth, take a walk past tumbling waterfalls and over the open fell to Eel Tarn before returning to Ravenglass by train.

There cannot be many historic inns that were set up as late as 1974. The Ratty Arms' building, however, dates from the construction of the Furness Railway in the 1850s, having been converted from old waiting rooms but with the addition of a substantial conservatory. There is also a patio, which is a very popular eating area when the weather is suitable.

The food is well cooked and varied, with fish, meat and vegetarian dishes all on offer, also baked potatoes and a carefully planned children's menu. It includes plenty of the healthy options that are essential these days.

Sandwiches, tea and coffee are popular with walkers and the choice of beers is wide. Telephone: 01229 717676.

- **HOW TO GET THERE:** Of all the walks described in this book, this one is unique in the sense that a train journey is an integral part of the route. It starts and finishes at Ravenglass station on the Ravenglass and Eskdale Railway (telephone: 01229 717171). To reach Ravenglass, turn westwards off the busy A595 road linking Barrow with Carlisle, following the signs.
- **PARKING:** There is parking in the village and at the railway. The NCP pay and display area is large and there is also parking on the opposite side of the main line railway. Travel up to Dalegarth on the narrow gauge railway (a journey of around 40 minutes) to reach the walk's starting point.
- **LENGTH OF THE WALK:** 3½ miles. Map: OS Explorer OL6 (inn GR 085966).

THE WALK

1. Explore Ravenglass, which in Roman times was known as Glanoventa. It was established as a port as early as AD 79 and a road led uphill and down dale to Ambleside via the substantial fort at Hardknott. The Furness Railway drove its line through the heart of the village in the 1850s, and Ratty was built in 1875 to carry iron ore and quarried stone from the Eskdale valley to the main line. A small but impressive museum tells the story of the railway and its associated industries. Nearby is Walls Castle, which is a strange name because this is not a castle but a well-preserved Roman bathhouse.

Having studied the timetable, join the visitors on Ratty and alight at Dalegarth station.

2. Again, consult the timetable. This is wonderful walking country and care needs to be taken not to go further than you intend – to be stranded here would involve a walk back to Ravenglass of 6 miles.

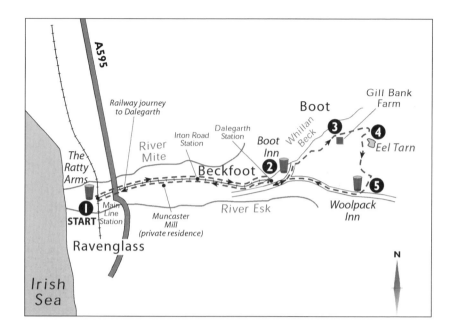

Take the road from the station and turn left to reach the village of Boot. Here is an 18th century packhorse bridge, which leads to a restored water-powered corn mill dating back some 600 years. Look out for a gate leading up onto a track following Whillan Beck with its attractive waterfalls.

3. Around the waterfall area look for Gill Bank Farm. Care needs to be taken here despite the recent Open Access ruling. Gill Bank is private but, before the gate to this, join a path which turns gently right and then left. At this point there is no confusion because the route is well marked and leads steeply upwards onto an open fell, with the Wasdale mountains ahead. Cross a feeder stream to the Whillan Beck. Turn right and follow a line of strategically placed stones.

4. Approach the pretty little Eel Tarn, obviously thus named because it once provided this fish for a hungry and protein-starved population. In the summer the tarn is full of colourful waterlilies, the broad leaves of which provide resting places for dragonflies. To continue the walk, descend steeply along a path marked all the way along by a line of white stones.

Ride on the narrow gauge railway to join the start of the walk

5. Approach a minor road on which stands the Woolpack Inn. Turn right and walk along the road to Dalegarth station. Return on La'al Ratty to Ravenglass. At the station it is possible to purchase a book of walks based around the railway and written by Alfred Wainwright.

A look to the west at the end of the day can provide a spectacular sunset over the Irish Sea.

20 Burgh-by-Sands
The Greyhound Inn

Students of Hadrian's Wall often make the mistake of just following the line from Carlisle towards Newcastle. The wall, however, began on the banks of the Solway Firth at the point where the river Eden enters the estuary. This is just what is so haunting about this fairly level stroll, which leads through marshland that is one of the most important ornithological areas in Britain. What buildings there are have stones incorporated into their fabric taken from Hadrian's Wall. About halfway along the walk there is a monument commemorating the military exploits of Edward I, surely England's fiercest monarch. On a more peaceful note the views across into Scotland and over the Solway are stunningly beautiful.

It is strange to find such an impressive hostelry in such a tiny hamlet. The Greyhound Inn is situated off the road and is a fine example of Georgian architecture. Don't look for a fancy menu but it you want a substantial meal you will not be disappointed. The local pies are worth travelling a distance to enjoy and so are the Sunday roasts – and the chef does not ignore either children or vegetarians. There is a very pleasant beer garden to eat in when the weather is fine. Telephone: 01228 576579.

- **HOW TO GET THERE:** This is one of the most remote places in Britain but within driving distance of Carlisle. From Carlisle Castle take the Abbeytown road (B5307). This is not easy to follow so go slowly. At Moorhouse turn right along a very minor road to Burgh-by-Sands.
- **PARKING:** There is limited parking on the single street, close to the church, and at the Greyhound, but permission should be obtained if a car is to be left at the pub while you walk.
- **LENGTH OF THE WALK:** 4 miles. Map: OS Explorer OL315 (inn GR 325590).

THE WALK

NB: As with any marshland walk, care should be taken after heavy rain or when snowfall infills some of the deep gullies. This route should never be attempted during mist or after sunset.

1. Begin in the hamlet and enjoy viewing the buildings, including a thatched cottage with walls made up mainly of wattle and daub and

The impressive monument to Edward I, 'the hammer of the Scots'

89

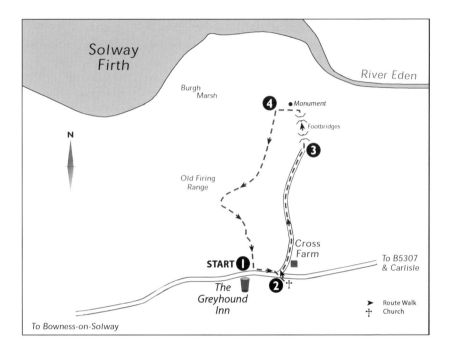

supported by substantial buttresses. There are also solid stone-built (from Hadrian's Wall) farms, which could be expected, but it is also surprising to see that there was once a tobacco processing factory within the complex of buildings. Continue to the church of St Michael. Here is an impressive pele tower built in 1181 – in the days when the Scots and English were in constant conflict – and constructed from stone taken from the Roman wall. The windows are narrow and the walls are almost 7 feet thick; this allowed arrows to be directed outwards but only the most skilful archer could direct a missile inside the structure. Look out for a memorial to Edward I whose body lay in state in the nave in 1307 (see point 3).

2. From the church turn left for a very short distance before turning sharp right. Follow a substantial track, which eventually leads into a damp area of marshland grass. At one time the sea-washed turf was exported for use in sports grounds, including Wembley Stadium during its heyday between the 1920s and the 1960s. This area is also something of an ornithologist's dream especially during the migration periods of autumn and spring, although winter watches can be marvellous. Look up to the right where at certain times of the day a spectacular bore rushes up the Firth and into the river.

3. This is a wet area and after turning left and passing across footbridges you reach the monument dedicated to Edward I. The ageing Edward, who had earned his name as 'the hammer of the Scots', camped on the marsh on his way to Carlisle from Lanercost in 1307. He was taken ill and died on 7th July. No monument was erected to celebrate his life until 1685 and a substantial replacement was erected in 1803. During a recent restoration an explanatory plaque was added.

4. The track turns left and passes through yet more bird-rich marsh, part of which was used as a firing range during the Second World War. It is now, thankfully, managed by the National Trust and is grazed by sheep and cattle, although stock numbers are controlled. The bird list is impressive here with curlew, redshank, oystercatcher and an amazing assortment of wildfowl, especially wintering geese. Cross little footbridges and pass over stiles and ditches and through gates to reach the road. Turn left and return to the village.